The Untold Story of Mary Magdalene

Matthew Robert Payne

Biblica, Inc.™

The opinions expressed by the author are not necessarily those of Christian Book Publishing USA.

Published by Christian Book Publishing USA.

Christian Book Publishing USA is committed to excellence in the publishing industry. Book design Copyright © 2019 by Christian Book Publishing USA. All rights reserved.

Paperback ISBN: 978-1-925845-10-5

DEDICATION

I want to dedicate this book to Jesus who makes us all the very best people that we can become. Jesus is a very real friend to me, and I pursue the kingdom and everything that it has for me.

TABLE OF CONTENTS

Mary Magdalene had a large business as a prostitute with wealthy clients, and she used to earn tons of money. In today's money, she would earn as much as $250,000 for a weekend with a man. She was a status symbol; she was the most gorgeous woman for thousands of miles; she was possessed by the enemy, and she had supernatural wisdom, knowledge, and beauty. Men spent $250,000 on her just to be seen with her. She was used as a status symbol. Rich billionaires in today's money would say to the other billionaires, "I have Mary this weekend. The party will be great because she'll be with me."

Mary was convicted by Jesus. Jesus preached these Holy Spirit messages to her; she used to turn up in disguise to listen to this famous teacher. Jesus used these messages to convict her. The first time she appeared, she noticed something in Jesus. Jesus looked directly in her eyes, and he was the only man who didn't lust after her. He was different. The first glance from Jesus wasn't filled with lust. She was used to sensing lust from every man; every man who previously looked at her had lusted after her.

When Mary turned up the first time, Jesus stopped preaching because he was led by the Spirit and by the audience, and the audience of one had turned up. He started preaching a really heavy-hitting message of repentance to Mary. Mary had enough money; she could take a year—even years—off without working. She could retire as she had land and properties and was very, very wealthy. Men paid a lot of money for her services. She had studied under the best philosophers and gone to other countries to sit under great teachers. She'd heard how good this man Jesus was and had come to see him for herself.

He was a great teacher. She had heard that he was fascinating to listen to. Mary showed up, and Jesus preached a convicting message to her. The first time she saw him, she walked away weeping. She came to see him again, and he did it again, and she wept and had to leave. Finally, she was broken; she went to a bar and got herself what we would call tipsy. But she got more than tipsy; she got pretty smashed to build up the courage to confront

Jesus. Then she went to the Pharisees' house and came in and wept on Jesus's feet, hoping in her heart that he could forgive her. She knew he was a prophet and that he knew all about her. Every one of his messages had illustrations all about her. She knew he was a mighty teacher and holy man, and he hadn't lusted after her like all other men did. She just hoped against hope that he would accept her.

She was one of the richest and wisest women that people had ever seen. The Jezebel spirit is very smart. She had might and was mighty; she commanded respect and had power through her wealth. She used to be carried around in a carrier with four extended poles. Kings and queens were carried around on these types of carts.

When she first showed up, she disguised herself before Jesus. As soon as she sat down, the whole crowd turned and said, "It's Mary. It's Mary; the great sinner is here to listen to Jesus." She was so ashamed; she was embarrassed that people recognized her. She went to great pains to dress herself down so that people wouldn't know who she was. She was embarrassed.

Then Jesus said, "It's not your riches; it's not your wisdom; it's not your might that counts in the end. It's whether you know the loving God who exercises justice and mercy in the world. That's what counts: your relationship with him."

Jesus quoted this passage from Jeremiah 9:23–24. "Thus says the Lord: 'Let not the wise man glory in his wisdom, let not the mighty man glory in his might, nor let the rich man glory in his riches; but let him who glories glory in this, that he understands and knows Me, that I am the Lord, exercising lovingkindness, judgment, and righteousness in the earth. For in these I delight,' says the Lord."

Then he expounded on her riches, her wisdom, and her might and told her it was all useless. It was useless. He said, "Everything that you have, Mary, is useless. You don't know my Father. And if you knew my Father, you wouldn't be behaving like you are."

Mary had all these rich clients, guys like the Donald Trumps and George Soroses and the Bill Gates of this world, the movers and shakers with money. They used to travel from different countries to spend the weekend with her. She was a status symbol; they bragged about her. But after she repented and Jesus said, "Your sins have been forgiven," Mary was suddenly out of business. She had enough wealth to live many lifetimes with a simple lifestyle. She didn't care about wealth. She retired.

Soon enough, Jesus invited her to be one of his disciples and to travel with him. When Jesus asked her to travel with him, she questioned him, "Are you sure you want me to follow you?"

Jesus said, "Yes."

She replied, "I'll bring much dishonor to your name."

And Jesus replied, "I want you to come with me and let me worry about the dishonor."

The Bible says that Mary and the other women supported Jesus with their funds. It's amazing that women fill the churches in the world. But some men think that women are the most gullible; however, I feel women are more spiritually minded than men.

When Mary retired, her former clients no longer had an attractive, wise, smart, intelligent, beautiful woman to spend their weekends with and to go to parties and social functions with. They no longer had their date. Some of these men had been with Mary for years and years. They only went to official functions with her. She was booked years in advance. Suddenly these men didn't have anyone who was her equal to replace her. They were lost. They were ships without a rudder or a sail.

Then they found out that this carpenter and rabbi was leading Mary all around Israel, and she was spending time with him and being his friend. He didn't have the money to pay her for her company. The rabbi didn't have the money they had. He was poor compared to them. They could see a stronger relationship form between Mary and him than they ever had. They knew of his reputation and wondered to themselves what power he had over her.

They knew Mary had been to see the greatest philosophers, the greatest artists, the greatest speakers. They knew Mary was intelligent, and she knew how to choose great speakers. They knew she wasn't a fool. So this poor rabbi intrigued these rich men and their wives.

The Pharisees hated this young rabbi, but he interested these rich men, and they liked the idea that the rulers of Jewish faith, the hypocrites, didn't like this young upstart that turned over the tables in the temple. Oh, they heard all about how this young rabbi turned over the tables in the temple; they'd heard about this fiery preacher who dared to make a scene in the temple. (See Matthew 21:12–13.)

Mary left everything for this guy, and they were intrigued. Sometimes Mary would stop and talk to them, and they were amazed that she even talked to them anymore. When she stopped and engaged them, they asked her questions. They had a hundred questions about the rabbi and her new life with him. What was she doing? What was she learning? Was he really smart? Was he really this radical? Was he going to bring new leadership to Israel as the rumors said? Were they all going to be answering to him as king? They wanted to know about this rabbi who sounded as though he would be in control of the nation soon.

They were rich, and they had vested interests; they had money. They had businesses; they had power; they had control. They had an inside woman called Mary. She took the time to stop and talk to them for half an hour when Jesus was in town or when she was resting for the weekend. They would ply her with questions; she'd listen as twenty of them were talking and asking all about this rabbi. Some of them committed their lives to Jesus on the spot just from her testimony. Some of them followed Jesus, gave up their businesses, and were part of the crowds that Jesus preached to.

What kind of life qualifies you to be a preacher of the gospel? Surely a past as a high-class prostitute, surely that would disqualify you. And surely a history as a woman who had slept with nearly every powerful man in Israel and other nations would disqualify you. What makes this Mary so talked about by Satan some two thousand years later? In modern books, Satan talks about supposed royal lineages and how Mary and Jesus married, and Jesus didn't die on a cross, but they had children. Satan hates Mary. Why does he hate her?

One time, Jesus was in a garden. Jesus used to go to a quiet place to pray. Jesus and Mary had a very important conversation there.

Around 4:00 a.m., Jesus used to wake Mary, tap her on the shoulder, and they'd both go out to pray. They were very close. She used to pray to God, and she could hear Jesus praying.

She used to go out in the morning and listen to him pray and be there, present with him while he talked to the Father and received visions and future information about what would happen that day. He'd see everything in visions: the major things he was going to do in ministry. He'd go to heaven and have encounters with his Father. He'd see everything that the Father wanted him to do that day. Then he'd go out and start the day with the people and do everything that he'd already seen in advance.

Mary used to go there with him, and Jesus would wake her up to take her. Imagine being in that place and being the closest person to Jesus.

Mary was there one morning; she watched him pray as usual. She walked up to him when he got up and asked, "Are you ever going to marry?"

Jesus started laughing, and he replied, "I'm not going to marry anyone, not even you."

She wept because that was her dream. Jesus and Mary were very close friends. He was the only man who loved her for who she really was, not for what she could give him. He wanted nothing. She offered him all her wealth. He said, "Just supply me as I need it."

Jesus so forgave Mary that he allowed money from prostitution to finance his ministry. What about that? Is that complete forgiveness? Imagine being forgiven and then Jesus saying, "But I don't want any of your money because it's tainted."

The Messiah can totally forgive and can even take money from a prostitute. Criminals launder money; they put money through legitimate businesses to make the money clean, to wash it, so that they can spend it on cars, property, and material items. They wash their money. Imagine being so washed by the blood of Jesus that even your prostitution money was now suddenly clean.

Jesus relied on Mary. He relied fully on the Holy Spirit and on his Father, and yet as a human, he had a real need for a close friend. Not many people understand this. Solomon said in Ecclesiastes 1:18, "With much wisdom comes much sorrow" (NIV). When you know things that weigh you down, these burdens can make you tremendously sad.

Jesus was so wise, but he could be very sad. Jesus understood every Scripture and verse of the written Old Testament and what they meant in context.

Jesus knew the Scriptures, and he knew them so well that he knew everything that would happen to him. He understood how far away the Pharisees were from the Word of God and the will of God. He knew his Father intimately; by then, he was having encounters every day in heaven. He understood the past, the present, Israel, and the future of the world. It's all written in the Old Testament. His own twelve male disciples, not including Mary, one of the unwritten, unlisted disciples, didn't even understand that he was going to die.

The twelve closest to him and even his inner circle, the closest of all (Peter, James, and John) who went with him to the Mount of Transfiguration, didn't understand that he was going to die and rise again. They didn't understand it. The Jews thought that the Messiah would rise up and save the Jewish world.

The Pharisees, teachers, and rabbis were blind. Jesus understood all the error and understood that the heart of man was deceitfully wicked. (See Jeremiah 17:9.) He knew what would happen to him from the passage that prophesied the following: "The plowers plowed on my back; they made their furrows long" (Psalm 129:3). This referred to how the Romans would whip the back of Jesus.

I saw him in a vision once, fresh from the crucifixion, and he couldn't have lived through what they did to his back. Modern medicine couldn't have saved his life. He would have died from that.

He knew the torture he would suffer. His face was beaten so badly that he couldn't be recognized as a human. Isaiah 53 says that he was marred beyond human recognition after what they did to him.

So in the garden, he was with Mary, and she asked if she could ever marry him because she was his closest friend. He was tremendously lonely; no one really understood him. No one even understood his purpose, let alone knew the meaning of the Bible, the Word of God, the Old Testament. No one had his knowledge or wisdom, no one.

Mary was really wise, smart, and very intuitive. Once she was imbued with the Holy Spirit and was pursuing more information, and she had hundreds of questions. As a prostitute, you learn to become close to men by asking them lots of questions about their lives and their interests, and then you ask more questions after they answer. You continue with conversation related to what the men say. If you have a lot of time with these men, you just keep on asking questions, and the more you ask about their lives, their futures, their plans, and their dreams, the more they fall for you. The more addicted to and dependent on you they become. The more they love you, and the more they fall in love with you. The more they'd give their whole kingdom and much of their wealth to possess you.

She knew that because she had done exactly this hundreds and hundreds of times with the richest and most powerful men in

Israel and from countries around those regions. She was an expert, so when she met Jesus, she did what she had always done and asked him questions.

Here are some of the questions she asked:

- Why are things this way?
- Why does the Old Testament say that?
- What does that passage of Scripture mean, and is it true?
- Why did you say that, and what did you mean?

And she listened to him preach, and you can hear some of this story in the book *Mary Magdalene Speaks from Heaven: A Divine Revelation.* Mary listened to him preach, and he'd use three hundred scriptures to tell the people that were coming out to see him that the Pharisees had no idea what they were talking about and that they were blind guides. He quoted many Scriptures from the Old Testament.

He said, "The Pharisees teach this, but if you look at these other five Scriptures, they teach the opposite. The Pharisees teach this, but if you look at these three Scriptures, they teach the opposite of what the Pharisees do. Don't do what the Pharisees do. Don't listen to them. They're blind guides who will lead you into a ditch."

Mary said in that book that if the sermon was put up on a YouTube video, there'd be so many Scripture references playing on the YouTube video that you could hardly see Jesus's face. He was quoting so many Scriptures. The Pharisees felt they had to kill him because he had wisdom beyond anything they could say. Matthew 7:28–29 says that the people were astonished when Jesus had preached the Sermon on the Mount because he taught with such authority that they'd never seen before in the teaching of the scribes and Pharisees.

He was the very best and the most anointed speaker Mary had ever seen. She fell in love with him. She started out by asking him questions and ended up falling in love. She started out hungry, and Jesus loves hungry people. I have noticed, as a prophet, when I meet people with hundreds of questions that they're just so hungry, and Jesus really loves them. I feel his love for them in my spirit.

Jesus loved Mary; she was so hungry. She didn't have to rely on finances for the rest of her life. She wanted to live this life. She wanted to become like Jesus. Jesus walked with a glory on him that used to turn heads a hundred feet away before he arrived. People could sense Jesus; they could sense a presence approaching them from a hundred feet away. People would turn around and look for the source of his glory.

I've met Jesus in the flesh before, and when I sensed him, he was thirty feet away from me, and I turned around to see where the presence was coming from. I regularly saw angels and Jesus in visions, but this time, I wasn't seeing a vision. It was a man, and the presence was coming off him, and I knew it was Jesus in the flesh. He sat down, waiting in a line for food at the homeless hostel.

I said to my friend who was a Christian, "That's Jesus."

He said, "I know that!" Four of us who were Christians were staying at the homeless hostel at the time. We recognized that Jesus in the flesh had visited us.

Jesus had this presence and walked with glory. Mary wanted to walk with this glory; she wanted to know what Jesus taught. She wanted to walk how he walked so much so that when he left, she wanted to be able to walk in his glory.

Let us go back to the story. Mary asked him if she could marry him. She asked him whether he was going to be married, but she was really saying, "Can I marry you?"

He said he wasn't going to marry anyone on earth, not even her, and it broke her heart. It just seemed the saddest thing for her to hear. Since he was a rabbi, he could be married. She thought she qualified to be his wife. Her dreams were just crushed.

Then Jesus told her why he couldn't marry her because he would marry everyone who became his follower. They would all become his spiritual bride, and he would be the bridegroom. All the women and men of the world who follow him with their whole lives would become his spiritual bride.

He asked her, "You wouldn't want to stop all the other women from being my bride, would you?" She cried and said no.

Then he told her, "The reason I can't marry you is because I'm going to die; they're going to crucify me."

Then she wept for half an hour. Have you ever wept before and sobbed and sobbed so that you just lost control of yourself and could not get control? She sobbed and sobbed, and she just lost control. She didn't know how she could continue to live after his death. He was so young; he was only thirty-three. He was so young. She thought she had at least twenty or thirty years with him, of this glorious life traveling everywhere with no want for money, no want for sex, no want for anything, traveling around with her best friend who was just so wise and the best speaker, the best person who had shown her more love than anyone else. He was the best man in the world, and nothing compared to him.

She just couldn't stop crying; she just wept and wept and sobbed and sobbed. Then she cleaned up her tears, and he told her that he was going to be resurrected and that he was going to heaven. He would send his Holy Spirit to empower her to do everything that he did. The Holy Spirit would also provide communication so that she could talk to him at any time in heaven. He said he would also visit her. He promised this to all his followers in these verses: John 14:21 and 23 and in Revelation 3:20.

We know that Jesus visited Paul after the resurrection. We know that was after the forty days. And we know that it's possible for Jesus to visit, according to the passages we listed above. These passages say that you can meet God and Jesus.

Mary was the only one who understood that Jesus would die, resurrect, go to heaven, and set up his kingdom in heaven before his death. She was so hungry, and she had a hundred questions about that, so many more than I can answer in this short message. She knew so much.

Jesus died, rose again, spent another forty days on earth, and ascended. Ten days later, the Holy Spirit hit, and the disciples were commissioned to go into the world and preach the gospel with the power, the anointing, and the enabling of the Holy Spirit, with all the power that Jesus had. We know that something hit Peter because his shadow could heal the sick. Peter used to walk around Jerusalem in the morning, and people from all over the world used to lie down. (See Acts 5:15.) They used to come from many different countries and lie down, and Peter would heal up to two thousand people just walking down the streets and talking to the disciples every morning. He didn't lay hands on them; his shadow just fell on them, and they were healed. They just got on the right-hand side when he was walking one way and on the left-hand side walking on the way home, and they knew where to lie, and every morning there was a healing crusade.

Mary went where her heart was: to all her friends who were her former clients. All prostitutes can have friends that are clients. When she was filled with the Holy Spirit, she went to her mission field, and she preached the gospel with signs and wonders following. People with sickness were healed; people who hadn't experienced extraordinary agape, unconditional love were shown that love by Mary. She converted a lot of these wealthy clients and their families.

Can you imagine someone with such inroads and such anointing and such connections that she could come to this world and preach the gospel to the richest men in the world? Can you imagine someone with this type of influence that could convert eighty of the top hundred richest men in America? Can you imagine what wealth would pour into the kingdom if that happened?

Mary opened up the gospel to the rich and powerful in her day. She not only ended up with enough wealth to provide for herself for the rest of her life and many lives after, but she converted the wealthiest men of all the countries to the way of Christ. As a highly intelligent, highly anointed woman full of glory, Mary turned her world upside down. People could sense Mary approaching a hundred feet away like they could sense Jesus. They knew Mary was coming before she even knocked on their door. They were out to greet the presence—the glory—that she carried.

She didn't just talk the talk; she walked the walk. She's the greatest untold story in the world. With all the time she spent with Jesus, she was one of the most qualified to preach the gospel.

Mary's influence in the early church has been a mystery ever since.

At one time, I knew this book was coming. I've always wanted to tell this story. I've met Mary two hundred times in visions, and she is one of my closest friends in heaven. She's sitting in my living room now, listening to the video as I record this. She is very proud of me. She loves the story as I am telling it and says that I'm telling her story so nicely.

I know a prophet who I highly revere, and I love his teachings. He consults with billionaires and millionaires. He says they can be a little bit stingy with their money. Billionaires don't get their money by talking a talk but by walking the walk. And they don't amass a lot of wealth by investing it in faulty systems. Billionaires don't make money by making stupid investments. Billionaires do their research. Billionaires invest in people, in visions, in dreams, and in ideas that look as if they will work. Billionaires take risks, but they don't invest in something that's wrong for them.

Billionaires don't invest in something faulty, so the reason that the modern church isn't attracting the wealth of some of the world's richest men is because they're not engaged in anything impressive. There's hypocrisy in the church. The billionaires can see how businesses operate, and they see that churches are running like businesses and charities, tax-free charities. Instead of the church, they often sow their money into charities that are doing a better job than the church in their field of expertise.

The billionaires in Mary's day had seen religion. What impressed them most about Jesus was that the religious leaders killed him. He was a threat to their system. If there was an equivalent to YouTube in those days, they would have watched every sermon that Jesus gave. Many of them went to the mountaintops, sat at the feet of Jesus and listened to him preach for days and days. But many of them just listened to Mary's testimony because she carried the glory. If they had a sickness, she could heal it. Mary didn't just talk the talk; she walked the walk. They loved her; they were already in love with her long before she met Jesus.

They were so impressed when they saw Jesus take Mary away; they'd all been trying to win her. Every one of them would have left their wives to marry Mary. Most of them had asked her to be their wife. These men were heavy hitters. Imagine if Mark Zuckerberg, the CEO of Facebook, asked a single female to marry him; so many women would give anything to marry such a rich man. They had power and control, and they would have dropped everything for Mary.

Then here comes Mary, and she is as good as this Jesus. She needs no preparation; she knows all the Scriptures; she can sit down with a scroll and tell you what every verse means. She's had long discussions with Jesus about every verse, and she was captivating to listen to. And she listened to everything and had this photographic memory. She was so wise, and she just applied all the truths of the Bible, everything of Jesus. She applied everything prophetically with the wisdom of the Holy Spirit to these business people and wealthy men's business lives.

She prophesied over them and gave them business and competitive strategies. She mentored these businessmen. Many of them just gave up their businesses and became full-time followers of Jesus and wanted to be like Mary. These men brought a lot of their wealth and laid it at the apostles' feet and financed the move that spread the gospel all around the known world.

I know Satan never forgot Mary. They're still making movies and trash books about Mary and Jesus and their supposed secret love affair. It's true; Satan always says a portion of the truth. No woman loved Jesus like Mary, and Jesus loved no woman like Mary. No one was closer to Jesus than Mary. It's all based on the truth. If they could have married, if it had been the Father's will, they would have married, and now they are married in heaven. She is now his bride as we all are his bride.

If we follow what Jesus teaches, if we become a servant, then a friend, then a son, and then enter into intimacy, we can be his bride too. But not all Christians are even followers, and not all Christians in the world are servants. So many Christians don't even know what Jesus taught, so how can they follow him? Not many become friends and know the secrets of Jesus. I'm a friend of Jesus; I'm a friend of God. Not many are walking in sonship, power, anointing, and authority in the kingdom. Not many progress from that to be the Bride of Christ.

I'D LOVE TO HEAR FROM YOU

One of the ways that you can bless me as a writer is by writing an honest and candid review of my book on Amazon. I always read the reviews of my books, and I would love to hear what you have to say about this one.

Before I buy a book, I read the reviews first. You can make an informed decision about a book when you have read enough honest reviews from readers. One way to help me sell this book and to give me positive feedback is by writing a review for me. It doesn't cost you a thing but helps me and the future readers of this book enormously.

To read my blog, request a life-coaching session, request your own personal prophecy, or receive a personal message from your angel, you can also visit my website at http://personal-prophecy-today.com. All of the funds raised through my ministry website will go toward the books that I write and self-publish.

To write to me about this book or to share any other thoughts, please feel free to contact me at my personal email address at survivors.sanctuary@gmail.com.

You can also friend request me on Facebook at Matthew Robert Payne. Please send me a message if we have no friends in common, as a lot of scammers now send me friend requests. As of November 2018, I'm starting an online church community via Zoom conferencing software, and I invite you to contact me to become part of this church.

You can also do me a huge favor and share this book on Facebook as a recommended book to read. This will help me and other readers.

HOW TO SPONSOR A BOOK PROJECT

If you have been blessed by this book, you might consider sponsoring a book for me. It normally costs me at least $1,500—often more—to produce each book that I write, depending on the length of the book.

If you seek the Holy Spirit about financing a book for me, I know that the Lord would be eternally grateful to you. Consider how much this book has blessed you, and then think of hundreds or even thousands of people who would be blessed by a book of mine. As you are probably aware, the vast majority of my e-books are ninety-nine cents, which proves to you that book writing is indeed a ministry for me and not a money-making venture. I would be very happy if you supported me in this.

If you have any questions for me or if you want to know what projects I am currently working on that your money might finance, you can write to me at survivors.sanctuary@gmail.com and ask me for more information. I would be pleased to give you additional details about my projects.

You can sow any amount to my ministry by simply sending me money via the PayPal link at this address: http://personal-prophecy-today.com/support-my-ministry.

You can be sure that your support, no matter the amount, will be used for the publishing of helpful Christian books for people to read.

SIMILAR BOOKS BY MATTHEW ROBERT PAYNE

Great Cloud of Witnesses Speak

Mary Magdalene Speaks from Heaven: A Divine Revelation

Mary Magdalene Speaks from Heaven Book 2: A Divine Revelation with Nicola Whitehall

ACKNOWLEDGMENTS

Jesus:

I want to thank you for being my lifelong friend and for never deserting me, no matter how dark my life became. You led me into some great adventures with saints and helped me compose this book.

Holy Spirit:

I want to thank you for leading and teaching me. You are a great teacher, better than I could ever be. You have been with me every step of the way. You had a lot to do with this book of mine, and I am thankful for that help.

Father:

Thank you for loving me and entrusting me with this life that I am living. Thank you for revealing my purpose to me and leading me toward accomplishing it. Thank you so much for your Son, Jesus. Thank you for everything that you have done in my life.

Lisa Thompson:

Thank you, Lisa, for editing this book of mine. You take my simple words and transform them to make me seem smarter than I really am.

If you have any editing needs, contact Lisa at *writebylisa@gmail.com.*

Friends:

Thank you, Darla, Lisa, Nicola, Mary, Wendy, Laura, David Joseph, and Michael Van Vlymen for your friendship and for how you have impacted my life.

Mom and Dad:

Thank you, Mom and Dad, for all the love that you have given me. I am a product of your love.

Readers and ministry supporters:

Thank you, dear readers. Thank you, ministry supporters, for the funds that you have given me to publish books. I live to educate people, and I thank my readers and the supporters of my ministry because you make life worth living.

ABOUT MATTHEW ROBERT PAYNE

Matthew Robert Payne, a teacher and prophet, enjoys writing what the Lord puts on his heart to share. He receives great pleasure from interacting with others on Facebook, hearing from people who have read his books, and prophesying over people's lives. He is a passionate lover of and disciple of Jesus Christ. He hopes that as you discover his books, you will intimately come to know Jesus, the Father, and Matthew through his transparent writing style.

Matthew grew up in a traditional Baptist church and gave his heart to Jesus Christ at the tender age of eight years old. But he left home at the age of eighteen, living a wild life for many years and engaging in bad habits and addictions. At twenty-seven, he was baptized in water and, at the same time, baptized in the Holy Spirit. Matthew learned about the five-fold ministry offices and received a revelation of their value today.

He started his journey as a prophet twenty years ago, learning about this gift and putting it into practice. With thousands of prophecies under his belt, he can confidently prophesy to friends and strangers alike. He has been writing for a number of years and self-published his first book in 2011. Today he spends his time earning money to self-publish and writes a new book approximately every month. You can find sixteen hundred videos of his on YouTube under Matthew Robert Payne.

You can connect with him on Facebook. You can sow into his book-writing ministry, read his blog, receive a message from your angel, or even receive your own nine-minute personal prophecy from Matthew at http://personal-prophecy-today.com.

Blurb

Many people are fascinated with Mary Magdalene. Over the years, I have interacted with Mary many times. As a result, I have learned the untold story of Mary Magdalene, which reads a little differently than what many popular books or media portray.

In this short book, see a bird's eye view of Mary: her life before she met Jesus, the life she had when she met Jesus, and the life she lived after Jesus left earth.

Read about the impact that Mary made on her world and on the early church and why Satan continues to make up dreadful stories about her even to this day.

This truly is the untold story of Mary Magdalene.

www.ingramcontent.com/pod-product-compliance
Lightning Source LLC
Chambersburg PA
CBHW020443030426
42337CB00014B/1365